Gallery Books
Editor: Peter Fallon

THE REED BED

Dermot Healy

THE
REED BED

Gallery Books

The Reed Bed
is first published
simultaneously in paperback
and in a clothbound edition
on 9 November 2001.

The Gallery Press
Loughcrew
Oldcastle
County Meath
Ireland

ISBN 1 85235 299 X (*paperback*)
1 85235 300 7 (*clothbound*)

The Gallery Press acknowledges the financial assistance
of An Chomhairle Ealaíon / The Arts Council, Ireland,
and the Arts Council of Northern Ireland.

Contents

THE REED BED

A Ball of Starlings

for Seamus Colreavy

As evening falls
over the bulrushes

parties of starlings
arrive in flurries

to join the other shape-makers
at the alt. The swarm blows

high, dives out of sight
in a beautiful aside,

till there's scarce a trace
of a bird —

then a set of arched wings appears,
then another,

hundreds turn
as one,

and suddenly over the lough
a whispering ball of starlings

rises into
the blue night

like a shoal of sardines
gambolling underwater

and, changing shape,
the birds

rise in the vast dark
like hayseed

till the puff-ball
explodes

and the birds
suddenly flip

again into nothingness:
and when the roost reappears out of the deep

in a great teeming net
of birdsong

the din grows intense
as they build

these last perfect
arcs, these ghostly

gall-bows,
before making

one final sweep
that ends

in a ticking globe
above the reeds;

then, chattering, the starlings spill
across the black fields.

When They Want to Know What We Were Like

When they want to know what we were like
they will search for the barriers we raised
against the wind. Aggression and erosion will place us
exactly. The way our battery walls faced
will tell them the direction
of the worst storms. A grave will be a windfall
for the weathermen. Our skeletons
will have a tilt to the spine
on account of walking head-down,
our lungs be huge from shouting in gales.
And everything they find will have been
somewhere else to start with.
How far have the cereals been blown
from the field in which they were sown?
And what of the moments of calm
that have been scattered over the wide acres?

The Purging

The sea would rot
if it didn't rise.

All that spring cleaning!
All that washing away,

night and day,
day and night,

of what the rivers carried
down from the mountains.

And then at last
the drying. The lying still.

The crackle of a sheet.
The whispering water.

The towelling breeze.
See at the bar

after the purging
the new man

water-mirrored
with the moon in his lap.

All the Meteors

Yesterday there were
things to be done.
Now, nothing.
It closes in.

All the meteors
have landed.
Six swans cruise
through the dark

and though I can sense
their cold-webbed feet,
the ruffled water
of the dark flood,

the whole thing is a blur.
I'm pinned
down here in a wind
from the south

among the wooden poor
of Ecuador,
the hee-hawing ass,
a dog,

a limping cat,
and whatever in the wide world
awaits me
after that.

I Catch Sight of Them as I Often Do

I catch sight of them as I often do
by chance, these stars,
these settlements of light,
and looking up last thing last night
I realised that just as their light
is only now reaching us, long after
they have gone out of existence,
where I now stand others have looked up
that are long gone.

They too
have gone out of existence,
these sea-folk who stored stars
in their heads for direction
and prayer;
the light from the stars
that reached them reaches me,
their existence shines down on my head
though they are long dead.

The light they saw then
is the light I see now,
and the light they saw then came from others
further back, looking up, like them,
like me, and the next to come after me;
and so on . . . the light of our lives
shining down on some other
who by chance looked up
before turning in for the night.

The Longing

The wide skirt of damp rock
on the giving tide.
Myself uneasy at the mirror.

I fight the longing.
This sick longing
enters me.

I have been amiss.
I better stop out of town.
All these fragments

weigh me down.
I do not want to go on
because you will not

be with me.
Above our heads,
above our heads,

the lightning
is searching the dark
for one perfect opening.

Away with the Birds

Just before a long journey
I get so homesick
that I can hardly talk,
or think, or eat,

all those half-heard notes
of transience
gather, the sough
and regret,

till this, I think with a start,
may be forever.
I'm so glued to this place
I get light in the head

at the thought of being elsewhere.
This time Hartnett
won't be behind me
on the plane

to spray water on.
The lungs will be gripped
by the ribs like claws.
A gin or two in the air

won't make up for the small habits
of every day. I'm finished.
Life will go awry.
And then there's the faces

of people saying goodbye.
Do they not see the fate
ordained for you?
The air-conditioners

going up into a whine
in some hotel where
last night's lovers are still at it
salaciously in your bed.

In a panic I launch
into something that will never
get finished, begin something
better left unsaid.

In the other room
you're putting away
trousers, shirts,
blouses, lipstick,

while in here
I'm pretending to work
the words when, in fact,
I'm away with the birds,

already sitting
out on the runway
at Kuala Lumpur
with a crossword

I began in Strandhill
and now half-way
round the world
I'm getting nowhere

wondering why I'm there
while I could be here,
and wondering why,
while I'm here,

I'm there already
by the southern ocean
beginning another round
of superstitions

to keep me going
and fill the distances between
the place I'm in
and the place I'm not,

not like in the old days
when I couldn't wait
to enter
the vast strangeness —

before first light
already on the road,
the thumb up,
the world before me.

Just Then

Just then I saw the earth below
with such clarity
that I forgot

my station in life.
Not a word about mortality.
No. Just these beings

generous to a fault
adding to existence,
then taking off

with their bag of tricks
and sores and complaints
and works and loves,

ponies, asses, dogs,
and that death rattle
which comes from the core

to leapfrog
into the memory of those
who will remember

them. With the passage
of time it's harder to get a mention
unless you're invented

again. Nothing doing
in the onion bed
or under the bonnet of the car.

Nothing stirring among
the blue bottles of Milk of Magnesia
for the bouts of indigestion.

The plastic shoes fill
with rainwater. The new crowd
are sitting in your chairs.

Things go on the same.
But there's hope —
at a wedding party

an old fogey — myself —
breaks out in tears
at the mention of your name.

The Hallway

Sometimes I find myself back in the bed I grew up in
floating there in the fever of adolesence

or if I'm not lying in that long bed
by Burke's whitewashed shed

more often than not I am down in the hallway by the hall-
    stand
where something is after happening.

It's unnerving to be so intensely young again.
Now youth is a nightmare from which I can't awake.

I'm back standing at the bottom of the stairs
at the half-glassed doorway onto the street

and outside the town beats like a cymbal.
I'm there most nights on the tiles,

high tide or low tide, or wherever I am
I'm back in the hall by the hall-stand

where the coats hang from question marks.
I am neither shadow nor substance.

It is not where you would expect to find yourself
after some years on the earth.

The house is dark and silent.
The door has just closed behind me or soon will open.

What darkness! What silence!

The Blackbird

I had great plans for the blackbird that came to live with us.
I'd camp out under his bush to catch his first stirrings, the
    first shout of 'I'm alive' to her,
'Is there anybird else out there?
I'm alive, listen . . . '

Then, as he shunted through his tunes, I below would hear
    him ask
his mate what she would like to hear, Would she like to hear
    the one I learned from my father,
and he from his?,
that dawn spurt

of delicious notes about jealousy, dreams. Do hear me, mate?
    Do you hear me, mate?
I mean it, Forgive me, Fasten the bow, Loose the sail, Eat the
    fruit, Tip the scales, Accept the shock,
and all that questioning
of the resolute heavens,

you heart, scald-lady, Do you mind, Do you mind how we
    were separated in November
by somebird, by somebird, How the wind cleaves, Him
    getting wilder in his confessions,
then the sudden silence,
and the quiet shame.

In my bed at five, I heard him step out of his nest and charge
    his trilling bill with joy.
At sadness, heard him pluck, scold, stop, teeter, sway, call in
    the animals at sunset
whistle for the fun of it,
and the forgetfulness.

He's on the gate with a stiffening tail-feather tilted like a
toothpick looking east.
He's gone, I think. The blackbird's gone, I say. Then, next
thing, I hear a song must be his.
There she is scuttling,
yellow-beaked, into the shadows.

The whistling blackbird, first to stop in this bare place, has
planted trees and rose hedgerows.
She's set seeds. He's tilled, trimmed, brought in a harvest of
treesong from way inland.
He lifts the stonechat's heart.
He silences whitearse

when *londubh* assails the coming dark with all the words we
have ever heard said in anger,
in love, he loves the quick of it timing every last refrain as
the sun is leaving Jimmy's window
When the bird stops
Suddenly. Suddenly.

For days I listened but it was too late. They're gone, I'll
never camp out below their song.
I lost my chance. I had a river at the bottom of my garden.
I had a lake, a pool.
I had a high tree, I had the warmth of a high tree,
I had a spring that emptied into memory.

Tongs

My mother sits by the grate
with a newspaper pressed
like a sail sheet
against the tall tongs.

Behind, the fire whooshes
as the draught ascends.
When the flames have taken
she lifts her feet

onto the lower mantel,
legs splayed neatly
before the open hearth.
She drops asleep

without her glasses on, mouth open
like a singer taking
a breath, and the hands in her lap
form a cup

into which passing strangers
might have put
some small token.
She is sleeping

between shifts.
Her chair is tilted.
One little toe in the brown nylon
is bandaged.

On the green fire-tiles
her two shoes.
In the nook the long-legged tongs.
On the window the bars.

When We Talk of What's Out There

When we talk of what's out there
inside us the real thing goes on
being said. 'Will you stop your snivelling,'
the dying woman said to the husband by her bed,
'you're making a fool of me.' Then she went off
to the place she feared most. And so the outpourings
of the normal save us from despair. 'The nights
are drawing in,' says a man as he looks
at his beasts. And what he means is all of this
won't last. 'Venus, I think,' the woman says, looking up,
but she might as well have said I have not slept
since John went. So do not speak of despair. Tell me
of one solitary object I can hold on to.
Give me its name. Watch how he sleeps,
the man who has cursed God.
He is holy and absolute in sleep.

Those Days

Those days
I could not pass a house
where a child was crying
without wanting to run.

Run where?
There is nowhere to run
after you leave a daughter,
after you leave a son.

And what have they lost?
A ghost typing
in the spare room
knowing that

with every year
an old tenderness
is fading. The early days
grow so distant they hurt,

and when we meet
it's like old people
who knew eachother
when they were young,

so far back
they have to begin
inventing it, that
awesome past,

and you think you
will never get over it,
the loss at your side
just here,

waist-level.

The Reed Bed

1

So it is with the reeds. I pass them daily
but the minute I've gone by

and the rustling stops
somewhere behind me

among the floating trees,
they no longer exist,

and then I start
wondering what is it I lost,

what was that thing,
that important thing,

I left behind me
on the dreaming road?

2

And then comes the moment
when returning home

I turn perchance their way
and there they are,

the familiars I lost
that morning,

sifting, by the dark tree
that marks the edge

of their watery bed,
a tossed acre of amber reeds

feather-headed,
frail, summoning.

3

And this is when
they truly exist,

when you come
upon them

at the last moment
and the eye

suddenly catches them
nodding in their bed

of cinnamon,
getting ready

in a flurry of whispering
to leave you again.

Only Just

1

. . . When night falls
the day passes
over Helen's child face

and she is back in a pram
or in a pink-laced cot
under a table,

there's washing in the air,
Saturday's midday news,
a plain ceiling,

then somewhere
near five
you toss suddenly

and scream
as they bury you
alive, in a wet grave . . .

2

. . . Wakening you
is like pulling someone
out of surging waters,

you flounder
with wild eyes
in the bed, say thanks,

and take my hand
and squeeze it
with trust,

then fall back in
to the deep
with a sigh.

The spear thrown
by ancestors misses
the sleeper, only just . . .

3

. . . Now your pillow is full of sleep
while mine is
awake all night.

Whoever the other fellow is
who dreams in me
he cannot be worse

than myself
when I cannot
rest. I'm on duty

at the gate
of a tremendous city
where complaints

and crazies
are on the go
till the early hours . . .

4

. . . When you get up
my shift is over. I fall
into your heat

and your shape;
above me is
the plain ceiling;

the news is on
in the distance. I slip
my head onto your pillow

to hear bird talk
from the garden
and what, for a second,

it is like to beat
in silence against
the wet coffin . . .

The Task

Go down into the dab with the rock,
I'm told, go down into the dab,

right down into the blue dab
is the job,

it's there you'll find
purchase for a wall,

man dear,
again' the say.

I'm down in the dab for hours
before I take a break to see

how far there is to go. Right
round the alt and on forever,

and I realise he's set me
a task for a lifetime, that man,

that man who sent me
down into the dab

to hoke
again' the ocean.

I tell myself be patient.
Carry smaller stones

but carry some.
Don't go,

you fool,
with nothing in your arms.

Chalkey's Grave

The moon came in on the ebb,
jib-sail aloft,

and filling fast
chased through

the blotted sky
sending every shadow

towards us,
raced across the troughs

and bar, the broken plough,
abandoned car,

as if this must be got
over with quick,

this torrid century
and the next:

then on her side
she stopped

to dock
a moment in

a flood
of winter

stars, everything
fell into

oblivion, the spade
moved back

from the house
and stood still

as sentinel
and dule-tree

at the spot in the garden
where I had

jammed it
into the dank earth,

not a bark to be heard
on the headland,

not a bark
from the house,

nothing, as the moon
passed overhead.

For a while
everything was upright,

then, as the shadow
of the spade's lean handle

started slowly back
across the garden

sheds and walls
went on the move,

the wee bare sycamore began
to climb,

the moon went in behind
a cloud

and doused the glim;
down, dog, down.

Then the moon swung above
my trousers on the line

and went beyond the vests
and shirts and turf,

the tin rooves
and lewing cows,

till, with sea-cloud trailing
in her wake,

at the alt
she took a look

at Horse Island,
lit the salt

in Moffit's field,
the wall of cockle

brightened
and the long shadow

of the gallows spade
crossed

the loose earth upon
the dog's grave.

It's done: turning west
she baled light

onto the Yellow Strand
and, lightened

of her load,
went on.

Who is That?

Who is that at the door?
The cat with a young lark in her mouth.

And that?
The thump of colour on a boulder.

Who is breathing?
Everywhere light is breathing fast.

It's breathing on gulls,
on ravens that stroll the burst sea-bed.

What is that on the sand?
The light that carries sound inland.

And the shriek?
The shriek is a warning.

Even the warm sun in the mist
is a warning.

Who is that at the door?
The cat with a young lark in her mouth.

A Warning

1

I see it happening
again, all that happened

last night,
numerous times,

many nights,
the same ravine,

the same attempt
to save myself . . .

2

Till I realise at last
that dreams

go over it
word for word,

that perilous descent
we make each night

to hear
the warning.

3

A warning has been
sent to me

from where things
happen over and over

and then once
only, and continues

even as I write
these words down.

Sunday, 16 August 1998

In Omagh
on a deserted street just after dawn
there was no one abroad
but some lone cameraman

taking a shot for the news. And at a slight incline
above the piled debris
the only thing still working
beyond his lens

was the traffic lights.
And there, though no car stirred,
the lights went red,
the lights went green,

and red, and green again;
for Stop, though no one stopped,
for Go, though no one went,
nor stopped, nor went again.

Undisturbed by all that happened
the lights still kept urging traffic
through the crack that opened
between ten-after-three

and eternity. And then they went faster
as if the bomb had damaged time itself,
then slowed again as if somehow they could
go back to normality.

Then faster still, the light for Stop,
the light for Go, the light for Stop,
the light for Go, the light for Stop,

for Stop, for Stop, for Stop.

Alas

In the dead house
pictures have been
turned to the wall
and the mirror
sheeted
with a pillow slip
in which
you can trace
the faint outline
of the sleeping head
that once lightly rested
there, and
the chant of prayer
rises for fear
we might hear
the unmilked cow
lewing in the flooded
haggard,
and again —
there it is —
the shake in the hand
of the bereaved
repeating itself
as she steadies
her fingers
upon the forehead
of the beloved
like someone, alas,
finding
balance

The West End

in memory of Douglas

Good day, mister, I say.
Good day to you, sir, he calls back
and salutes, a sharp snap of the full hand
to the forehead, then we trundle by eachother
on the beach road.

And this went on for several winters,
the salute, himself and his dog, and after that dog
another, the two of them braving sleet
and churlish wind,
and he always calling me sir!

Sometimes I'd meet him dropping into Ellen's
for crisps and fags. And heading West
he'd lift his bald terrier to let a car pass.
After the worst storms he'd appear on the road
carrying shopping home.

Then one day I learnt that he had worked
next door to me in Picadilly years before
and so I stopped up to tell him the news.
He looked at me for some time.
Are you the author? he asked.

I am, I said. So what happened, he said,
that we found ourselves in this dreadful place?
The want of wit, I think, he said,
and he headed off to his caravan
in the dank West.

And so for some years here we were
far from Eros and all the girls,
the Classic cinemas, the strip joints,

hamburger stalls, the French House,
Wardour Street, Ward's,

of no consequence to each other
except for that co-incidence in the sixties.
We share a past, mine more sordid than his
perhaps. Men from office days
in the West End

tipping outdoors when rain is finished
into another West where the murder of the sea
is news, or mud-wrestlers in Jordan's,
and now and then, a squad car on the dunes.
We know few here

except those we took with us.
Good day, sir, I call. Good day to you, sir, he calls,
and leans back and salutes
like a book that always opens
at the right page.

All Soul's Day, November 1998

The Words

The rain started slowly,
began with a single perfect drop

that took an age
to run down a page,

then came another and another
till the glass was streaming.

Soon the hail was peppering the lakes
and driving across the Atlantic;

a cloud-burst
struck the wide empty desert;

a bullfrog
sang,

and the first words
issued from

the throat-singers.

A Sober Night with Stars

A sober night
with stars,

one swift clean bell.
The copy

send to heaven;
the original

leave in hell.

Plants, Heavy with Berry

Plants, heavy with berry,
in a frost. Not far off,
a house.

A voice, a reason.
A kitchen. Exhausted by choice,
I lie awake

and rise worrying
the same tune,
sit looking for an opening,

then empty-headed
while away the time
with cards

or crosswords,
looking up and around me
as people will

who search for words
and feel ridiculed
by what they do,

beside the muffled Atlantic
or in some city
in mid-afternoon,

looking up and around
as if someone were
watching them,

these malingerers,
afraid of the what-not, then
conscience-stricken

I come to my feet.
Time to go shopping, man, weed
the blasted garden.

Manure the drills,
do your shoes, clear
the walls of lichen.

Not far off, a house.
A voice, a reason.
A kitchen.

The Strange Impasse

So many things happen
while you are looking the other way,
it's better that you don't know,
can't know; leave it,
forget it, it's not your business,
and of course you get angry over nothing,
then give over. Read without taking in the words,
nod at what you don't hear,
turn aside and have another beer,
could you say that again, sir?
Again, please, I was elsewhere.

Or maybe it's the news and you're
looking straight at what is not happening,
because it will be repeated again
ad infinitum. On the Six or the Seven
another dumb outcry not your own.
Could I have that again, sir?
Daydreaming, when someone is telling you
exactly what they've seen or done;
you're travelling the world in first class,
decrying, in an awkward silence,
that human engineering should lead
to this strange impasse.

The Whispering Shells

for Inor

1

The tide mark
in March

is not seaweed
or shale

but a breathless
line of shells

filled again
with voices

wandering the ward
at nightfall.

2

The sea they hear
is a field of insects

shunted through
all the senses.

The boat they're on
sails through

my mind, and my mind
founders

out there
on the hush.

3

The lost
are looking

for a break
in the weather

as they bale. They pray
to get better

at landfall,
tomorrow, the day after,

dear God, when
they might look

with wonder
on sanity again.

4

The oarsmen
are rowing

towards deliverance
from despair

as they paddle the deep
waters of the unnamed,

they sight land
that is not land

but a heave of water that slowly banks high
into cloud and falls down there again.

5

Each man in his cot
calls out

to his fellows —
and back

come their
awesome replies:

I am out here forever.
There is none

to deliver me. And is there nowhere
after this?

6

They search
the empty ocean.

They enter
the cuckoo storm.

The boat is
filled with blue salt,

the music board
shattered.

Sometimes it is too late
to be saved.

7

And then to draw closer
through the slough

of teeming sandflies,
to dock at last

at this strange
drunken coast

where the first thing
each man heard

was his own
whispering shell.

Walls

There was a time
I used marvel over
a green bottle or claypipes
set oddly into a stone wall.

Now that I've started
building them
I put everything in,
chains, plastic, shells.

I put in all
I can carry,
wheelbarrows of scraws and more,
if I can find it,

and sometimes
I panic in the windy
open spaces,
and often rest

where there
was nothing before,
and think, well,
the wall under me may lack

the Donlon touch,
the finish of mason and fiddlemaker,
saddler, farmer.
A poor type of man

I am to follow them
who built battery walls
and turned the earth
around to face

the north-west.
So be it.
I look back,
pleased with myself,

as if I'd just climbed
Everest
and was waiting for
the others to arrive.

The Wall I Built

The wall I built
the sea took.

The stones I gathered
the sea scattered.

Falling asleep I look
left, right,

because, you see,
they don't make

tomorrow like
they used to.

The Sky Road

for Dallan

A summer's night
we returned unseeing through fog
to the house

to find the mist had stopped
just at the front wall
and, turning back,

we found a glacier,
a long grave white floor
that you would be tempted to walk on,

reaching for miles,
to the prow of the mountain.
On all sides

down hung.
We might have been in a cave
where old dingoes

had ghosted to a standstill
and were trapped
in a frozen drop of hail.

To the left the sea had been swept into a corner.
The grey heads of trees stirred in shrouds.
A roof of a house shedding dew

floated by. And beyond that
an orange light that once marked something
marked nothing at all.

We were alone up there,
above cloud level.
Who slept underneath that bank of mist

did not exist. All landmarks were gone.
We were alone up there on Dooneel,
all sound off

except for the low cough of a cow out there in the stillness.
In front of me the shadow of my son
grows the length of me

and goes beyond me,
beyond our absences and our tempers
down this long white sky road,

this strange sea-bed,
blanketed in fog. No one. Not a stir.
The world down to a whisper.

What Happened at Noon?

What happened
was

all the cats
took off their caps

and looked out to sea,
the hares quit

the rocks,
the waves stopped,

and birdsong
suddenly ended.

Then the light
left me.

A Breeze

I step back from the crossword
and turn to see
the leaves of the dictionary
flap in the breeze

outside on the plastic table
in the gravel yard,
then as the winds increase
the large atlas starts unfolding,

till all the planets
and countries and words
and their meanings
are flying by

as if the books
were being flicked through
by some demented reader
who has lost his place

in the world:
shaman, shiite, shogun,
Mars, adverse, idiom,
to rebuff, to slander,

a fall of hail, vacant, volatile,
Saturn, Sierra Leone,
Azores, otic, wrack, Chad,
China, Cyprus, Rome;

the pages speed by like frames
in those early movies
till it all makes
some kind of story,

a new migration has begun,
the Sahara is crossed,
an oasis named,
the way we came forgot,

the wanderers leave
Gabon for Ghana
and at Jerusalem part
in various languages

to search for meaning again.
Sessa: an exclamation mark.
Jupiter. Limitrophe: on the border.
Hay: a dance. Hush: a rush of water.

Then the wind eases,
the mad search for whatever it was
stops. The breeze has reached
sermocination in Beijing.

The Cat

The cat who has lost her voice
is the cat that calls out loudest.

So it is when the muse goes
into the terrible silence.

Larkin's Room in a Storm

In the storms I imagine city rooms
where everything is laid out to the touch,

a seat by the window,
binoculars, wine glasses, so much

jazz. Everything in its place
like the first hand of a game of cards.

Outside, a breeze blows through the tombs
of the dead who died in Wandsworth.

A stranger looks into my face.
Wild cats flit through breakers' yards.

No one is hurrying. The single men are home.
And women stand with cup of tea in hand

watching Coronation Street in Camden.
In some square a computer comes on.

The fifth chapter of a novel is ending.
The Kirk family is spending

Easter on Mars.
I am on the top deck of a bus

that's turning through slush
down the King's Road in Chelsea.

In the manager's office of Pellet and Son
I'm the security man reading Dostoevsky.

It's after 12. It's Christmas Eve.
There's a taxi queue in Clapham.

By the old King's Head someone shouts,
'Let me go, just let me fucking at him!'

The rain has stopped. It turns to snow.
We travel on drugs through Pimlico.

A Henry Moore sits by the Thames
but acid does not go art.

Instead we marvel at the shining plinth
and coming back I fall apart

and there I do it again
throwing myself into the traffic

on Vauxhall Bridge
and wake up in Wicklow

in a shed of flea-bitten hounds.
I stand by the sea with the mange.

Everything I look on for years
is permanently strange.

I find myself at a table
eating bacon in Ward's

Irish House. Once again on a bus,
or a tube, or a street, going

past rampant TVs, booklined walls,
Italian shops, Italian stalls,

The Queen's merc stalls in the dark,
the ducks are leaving James's Park,

I'm woken by reggae
in Caldwell Street,

it all comes back,
the arguments, the loss,

then suddenly here I am
in a room by the sea

in blinding sleet
away from all the harm.

And yet I'd like to aspire
to a centrally-heated library,

like Larkin, in rooms where fires
come on at a touch

rather than flailing in the dark
through a stack of turf,

and like him at his best
be thinking of death

after another night of sordidness.
Alone. Vexed.

Better to be abrasive in Hull
than go shouting 'Go fuck yourself!'

to no one in particular
on a windy peninsula.

One Minute with Eileen

1

After finishing work
I take a shortcut through Soho

and pass an open door
that says: two pounds

for one minute with Eileen.
Well, I ponder this,

then turn and turn about.
The old lady behind the counter

gives me a blue ticket.
Sit there, she says, Eileen

is occupied at present.
I'll wait on the street, I say.

2

So I took a turn or two
through the Chinese,

like a man about
business in the town,

and soon enough, a youth
doused in gel emerges

head-down
like a duck in thunder

and high-tailed it
in a north-easterly,

and the lady waved me in.
The inside door opened and

I sit in an armchair
facing Eileen.

3

Now, she explains,
I'm a tipsy girl.

If you want to touch me,
that's twenty; if you want me

to touch you, that's forty.
Full sex is sixty.

Anything after that
is over a hundred.

And what, I asked,
do I get for my two pound?

You get to hear the prices, she said.

Wonderers

I find myself looking
across at your face
wondering

for the umpteenth time,
who you are,
where you came from,

and then, as always,
begin wondering
who this is,

who is this
that wonders who you are?
And from your face

I can see that for a moment
you too have forgotten who I am.
How strange

I must be to you
who thinks he knows
you best of all,

how strange you are to yourself,
how strange we all are
to ourselves and others;

like those folk you see in photos
waiting at train stations
for familiars to arrive,

folk seated in places
with their hats
on the seats

beside them;
and moments later
these strangers

on the seats beside them.
They fall into each other's step,
take the same breath

as they cross the bridge
to the monument
and, laughing, make it home

at last; then somewhere
in the kitchen,
in the drenched garden,

comes the moment
when they realise
that the least

is known about the one
they love best —
we have been making each other up —

that look is made,
the look that
begs the question,

who are you
and who am I
and who are all the rest?

Reaching the Rockies

In the middle of a gale
with the peelers high
I found myself going back to Canada
in an old notebook I'd kept;

I turned the Apple on
and took a seat at the back of the plane
and was amazed again to find
that the steward serving food

was the spit of a gay dancer
I'd seen in Barcelona
break into tears
on the last night of the panto;

we're airborne, we're off;
to make the long journey
that leads back
to endless trivia:

Did Frank Brady meet
James Coyle the piper? And if they did,
did they get on? And so on . . .
while the air thins

over snow pitted with wind steps;
a lonesome white place,
sleeping in our consciousness,
as we sleep in it,

on a lake of white
these dark hoof-prints of wind
run, these thumb-prints,
toe-prints,

then the white turns windless.
The ghost animals stop.
All becomes the same above and below.
The line between blue and white sharpens.

And back to my right a Japanese couple,
with their eyes glued tight to the video screen
and their ears in earphones,
continue to play pontoon.

As she boxes the cards
he taps the table. She deals. He turns.
She deals again! Where am I?
I look out, look in.

In a blink I lost a hundred miles.
The ice cracks like weak tea
and civilization blinks on and off
like a bulb going.

The cracks make roads.
There's the glint of sun on aluminium.
The snow lifts like the skin of an ass
shedding winter hair.

A world of squares begins.
Ice cool in buckets.
A river is thrown onto the land
like a scarf left after the night before.

The rings of the jet
are silent, round, oozing power —
then the whole thing disappears.
Canada is gone.

I jump back in fright.
The computer gives with a start.
For a minute I sit suspended
high in the chilled air

till I realise the electricity
has given, a transformer is down somewhere,
and I'm left in crackling space
alone, in darkness —

just as we reached the Rockies
with nothing saved
and whatever happened after
never to come again.

Somerset Maugham on Bass with
The Harp Jazz Band in Enniskillen

for Roddy

The other night I came across
Somerset Maugham
playing his heart out
on double-bass and mouth organ

along with Spencer Tracy on piano
and a few other dudes
in a version of 'Ain't Misbehavin' '
in Enniskillen.

Somerset Maugham was huge and lived-in
and kept his eye on the bar;
Spencer on the other hand
kept time with his chin —

What a din! What a do!
Jazz in Orange Halls.
Jazz down The Falls where old pros turn
into old film stars,

then later, going home, I think of
this Somerset Maugham
lying down in his room
just before dawn

somewhere off the Crumlin Road
where old LPs line the walls.
He sleeps among the greats
and wakes hearing a tune

he fell asleep playing
in a small café
in the South of France, yes,
in Marseilles perhaps.

He is playing a tune for the cast of *Casablanca*
who just dropped in
on the off-chance.
He's away now with 'A kiss is just a kiss';

'A smile is just a smile',
he sings to the pimps.
Henry Fonda is on his feet.
Duke Ellington steps

out of the shadows
to applaud Maugham on mouth organ,
and the plane carrying the Glenn Miller Band
has not yet left the ground.

Father and Son

for Phil Lawlor

At any given moment of the day
my eye will light
on the plaster cast
of Joseph and Jesus

as they sun themselves
on the cluttered sill,
sometimes with their back to all
that's out there,

and other times facing towards —
snug in their robes —
the wine skies
and teeming rain.

He has him in the crook of his arm,
the hollow father,
and the child's fixed gaze
never wavers

from a point on Raughley
where the blowhole
is. Out of pagan China or Korea
they came

and they came in thousands,
this porcelain pair,
to look down from kitchen walls
in farthest Cracow,

to light up
when the driver strikes the brake
of taxis in Quito.
They are there

in the dark nooks of chapels
in Crete. With all the art about
you'd wonder how they persist
in being lovely.

The carpenter looks out
on the flooded fields —
fences of storm-tossed
fertilizer bags,

black plastic, nappies —
with the benign eye
of a man who has seen worse.
The red-haired child

is awake before anyone
else in the house —
up into his father's arm with him.
Last thing at night

the pair are there,
closer, somehow content,
with the father's skirt
hitched up,

and the hollow son smaller,
shadowed by the wide black
of all that is beyond
the reflecting glass.

They are watching
for the return
of the woman who's away
in Sligo town.

May she come soon,
that I do not resort to prayer!
I'll put them on the step outside
to guide her home.

First Thing

First thing in the morning
I saw a stoat
sloping along the turf.

Another member
of the extended family!
One morning soon

I'll glance out
and find an elephant in the surf
looking off into the middle distance,

and it'll only be a matter of time
before I've trained him
to lift stones

from the soft belly
of the wet flowing seaweed,
the yellow pods of sea-corn.

After him will come
tigers, ostriches, elks,
and we will make wonderful fossils,

all of us, woman,
cats, dogs, tern,
sculpted in time

beneath a maidenhead fern.